CW00739887

Seaweed Foraging
in Cornwall and the Isles of Scilly

Rachel Lambert

First published in 2016 by
Alison Hodge, 1a Gwavas Road, Newlyn,
Penzance, Cornwall TR18 5LZ, UK
info@alison-hodge.co.uk
www.alisonhodgepublishers.co.uk

ISBN-13 978-0-906720-97-4
British Library Cataloguing-in-Publication Data
A catalogue record for this book is available from
the British Library.

Edited by Yvonne Bristow

Designed and originated by
BDP – Book Development and Production,
Penzance, Cornwall
Printed in China

Title page: Seaweeds in a rock pool in West
Cornwall, including kelp, forest kelp, dulse,
thongweed and coral weed.

Some medicinal uses of seaweeds are
mentioned, though not extensively listed in
this book. Always seek medical advice from
your GP, health professional or medical
herbalist before using, and never self-
prescribe.

Note that, for ease of use, seaweeds in this
book are listed alphabetically by common
name, rather than by type.

Contents

Introduction

There is something about the underwater world of seaweeds that is intriguing, and of all the foraging topics that I teach, seaweeds seem to have the most allure. For myself, I'm not sure what it was that first drew me to them. Perhaps it was the ease of picking and identifying them, their abundance, their amazing nutritional qualities, or the sheer vitality of being down on the beach; the fresh salty air, the sound of the waves, and picking my own food.

Once you spend any time around a rock pool, a whole other world opens up. Staring into a pool there is an amazing array of colours and activity. Green weeds, brown ones, red ones, pink ones and white ones, ones with iridescent tips, and the potential of the unknown in the crevices and under rocks. At a good low tide, you can step out further into a world that is revealed, at most, twice a day. Closer to the depths, looking out to sea, you will find larger brown seaweeds, metres long, moving in the water or lying still against rocks waiting for the tide to enliven them again. Discovering the flavours and nutritious foods that lurk in these places between the rocks and under the sea gives your time on the beach a whole new, exciting dimension.

Seaweeds in Cornwall and the Isles of Scilly

Both Cornwall and the Isles of Scilly (IOS) have enormous access to the sea and seaweeds; indeed, both are among the most abundant areas for seaweeds not only in England, but also in Britain. Records show that the IOS and South Cornwall are very rich in seaweeds. These are also areas that have had a lot of study, enabling over 400 seaweed species to be identified in Cornwall out of approximately 640 species off the shores of the whole of the UK. The shores and subtidal (below the tide mark) areas of the IOS are known to support at least one-third of the red, green and brown species reported for Britain and Ireland. North Cornwall is probably richer than records show, for this is a difficult place to dive, and visibility is problematic.

Rock pools at Lean Point, near Treen Cove, north-west coast of Cornwall

One of Cornwall's important historical links with seaweeds is through John Stackhouse (1742–1819). Stackhouse was born in Probus, near Truro, and dedicated his life to the study of botany, in particular seaweeds and their reproduction. A common name for *Chondrus crispus* is Stackhouse, and there also exists a Stackhouse Cove in West Cornwall, both named after this man's pioneering research and illustrations.

Until recently, within the British Isles, Ireland, Scotland and Wales have led in celebrating their historical use of seaweeds as food, and in increasing their current use.

However, with many nationally acclaimed chefs and health experts singing the praises of seaweeds, and the birth of the Cornish Seaweed Company in 2012, they are now coming into the limelight in this south-west corner of the country.

Choice of Seaweeds

Seaweeds – referred to here as plants – are actually marine algae. Those off the coast of the UK amount to around 7 per cent of the world's seaweed population (Natural History Museum, London). That's a vast array available to us. All seaweeds, apart from the Desmarest's seaweeds (*Desmarestia aculeata*, *Desmarestia ligulata* and *Desmarestia viridis*), are edible, but not all are tasty or nutritious, with nutrients accessible to the human body. The *Desmarestia* seaweeds contain sulphuric acid, and when under stress or cut, this is released into the water, disintegrating other seaweeds nearby. It can severely upset the stomach. The *Desmarestia* family all grow between 0 and 10 metres below the low-tide mark, so avoiding picking and diving for unidentified seaweeds will avoid confusion.

In this book I have chosen to focus on sixteen seaweeds. Some have been known for their eating qualities for a long time; others are less well known. All are in good abundance in Cornwall and the IOS (but please follow the notes on sustainability, pages 10–12). I wanted to give as wide a range as possible, rather than just focus on the top ten. I have omitted sea noodles (*Nemalion helminthoides*) as it is not very common and quite difficult to work with in recipes. I also chose to omit the jelly plant (*Gelidium latifolium* and *Gelidium sesquipedale*), as despite being the chief source of agar (a well-used ingredient), it requires a lot of processing to extract it. Seaweeds you might have heard of, and which are included are bladder wrack, dabberlocks (kelp family), dulse, carrrageen, kelp, laver, pepper dulse, thongweed, green seaweeds (gutweed and sea lettuce) and sugar kelp. Finally, my inclusion of some seaweeds that are largely ignored for their edible potential was driven by my determination to widen my own understanding of seaweeds, our palettes and nutrition. These are channel wrack, egg wrack, green sponge fingers, mermaid's tresses and wireweed. I hope you enjoy my choice.

Eating Seaweeds

It may come as a surprise to you that I find seaweeds – sometimes known as sea vegetables – rather comforting in their taste; subtle and easily digestible, and somehow recognizable to my body if not immediately to my taste buds. Of course, I have met many people who shudder at the thought of them, whether looking at them, swimming among them, touching or eating them. Although I would always respect personal preferences, I would also challenge anyone who says, 'I don't like seaweeds'. Seaweeds are so varied

Life in a rock pool: Gutweed (Ulva intestinalis) and unidentified red seaweed

in their tastes and textures, it is almost like saying 'I don't like eating plants' – grains, fruit, vegetables, nuts and seeds. Whether you like salty, spicy, crunchy, juicy, soft, sweet or umami (what's known as the fifth savoury flavour), there's a seaweed for you. And that's just the raw seaweed; processing and combining them with other ingredients creates an infinite array of dishes to savour.

Seaweeds for Health and Nutrition

Seaweeds are a great source of nutrition, and are particularly popular and useful for vegans and vegetarians as they provide essential nutrients hard to get outside animal or fish/shellfish sources. Several seaweeds also have a good percentage of protein. Some seaweeds are better to eat in small amounts, as in a condiment rather than as a vegetable (see individual seaweeds). Equally, some brown seaweeds (see Seasonal Picking Chart on page 17, and individual seaweeds) are high in iodine, which is essential for health though needs to be consumed in moderation. Always seek medical advice, from your GP, health professional or medical herbalist.

How to Use this Book

As with my first book, *Wild Food Foraging in Cornwall and the Isles of Scilly*, this book is both an identification guide and a recipe book. It has essential information on safe, legal foraging of seaweeds (please read all of this and refer to it as often as you need), as well as notes on nutrition and tips on processing and cooking a variety of different sea vegetables. It is a practical guide, and aims to bring edible seaweeds more into people's everyday lives. All information included is considered of value and accurate at the time of print, and results from years of testing and researching.

The author leads a foraging walk in the Scillies

Law on Seaweed Foraging

In the UK a licence is needed to forage seaweeds commercially, and there is no common law granting you or me the right to pick them for personal use either. It is necessary to obtain permission from the relevant land-owner before removing growing or loose seaweeds.

However, as seaweed has been harvested for centuries, you may find that many land-owners will not be averse to small amounts being taken for personal consumption.

Beaches and the coastline in Cornwall and the IOS belong to the Duchy of Cornwall, the Crown Estate, a charitable body such as the National Trust, the Cornwall or Isles of

Basket of carrageen, sea lettuce and thongweed, St Martins, Isles of Scilly

Scilly Wildlife Trust, the local council, or a private landowner.

Furthermore, some areas have a protected status and require additional permission from Natural England in order to forage there. These are the Special Areas of Conservation (SACs), Special Protection Areas (SPAs), Marine Conservation Zones (MCZs), and Sites of Special Scientific Interest (SSSIs).

Safety and Sustainability

The sea is a powerful entity, and mixed with certain weather conditions can be highly dangerous. Natural conservation is equally of concern when it comes to seaweed foraging. The seas are changing, and many aspects threaten the seaweed population, including: climate change (global warming and increased storms), increasing human population and coastal human activities, acidification of the seas, food consumption and foraging – with warming seas and acidification thought to have the most impact on seaweeds.

Native seaweeds are suited to their natural environment, and as these changes increase, some – kelps, sugar kelp, dabberlocks, bladder wrack, channel wrack, egg wrack and thongweed, for example – are expected to decline, while others – mostly non-natives such as wireweed, green sponge fingers and wakame (the latter is not covered in this book as its recorded levels are currently too low in the UK) – are expected to increase. Reports imply that these changes have already begun in some areas, though further research is needed. The most obvious change is the increase of non-native species.

Seaweeds play an important role in our ecosystem, from providing habitat for a wide variety of species to forage in, feed off, spawn and nurse in, and a refuge from predators for fish and invertebrates, to assisting coastal protection by dissipating wave energy, capturing sediments and nutrients and providing a carbon sink. Thus care for these marine plants is essential for our wellbeing and that of our planet.

The following guidelines are therefore highly recommended, and are heavily in-formed by Natural England's (NE) seaweed-harvesting code of conduct.*

Seaweed Foraging Guidelines

- Consult NE and the local Inshore Fisheries and Conservation Authority (IFCA) before harvesting seaweeds. Always get the landowner's permission (council or private).
- Routinely check tide times and weather conditions before foraging; an onshore wind can bring in the tide unexpectedly fast, and weather conditions can change quickly. Never turn your back on the tide; it's best to forage as the tide is going out, and stop before it turns and comes in.
- Always cut seaweeds and keep the holdfast (a root-like structure that secures the seaweed to a surface) intact. Pulling them off unnecessarily breaks the holdfast and kills it. Use scissors or a penknife, or grip the seaweed firmly in place with one hand, and carefully tear it with the other. Do not use mechanical means or vehicles on the foreshore.
- Avoid disturbing wildlife such as seabirds and seals by keeping an appropriate distance away, and avoid or minimize trampling on other organisms, such as stalked jellyfish, brittle-stars, tiny moss animals (bryozoans) and blue-rayed limpets.

- Check your harvest for unwanted attached organisms before leaving the beach and before cooking, processing or eating. Wash seaweeds thoroughly to remove any debris or sand.
- Take extra care when picking invasive non-native species, to ensure spores are not spread to other areas, by following the 'CHECK, CLEAN, DRY' approach. Check equipment (for example, clothing and scissors) and your harvest, cleaning and drying thoroughly.
- Collect no more than one-third of each plant, and generally harvest small amounts, rotating where you pick.
- Harvest only what you will use. Drying seaweeds takes time and space, so consider this before cutting large amounts (see Drying and Storing Seaweeds below). Many types of seaweed have branches, and you can take some branches, leaving the rest of the plant intact.
- Harvest seaweeds during the growth season (when they can recover quickest) and after reproduction (see individual plant guidance on season), and leave a large proportion of mature plants behind.
- Pick only fresh, living and attached seaweeds, unless you are absolutely certain they are freshly broken from their holdfast (as is often the case after a storm).
- Forage from clean, non-polluted areas and beaches, and avoid or limit picking seaweeds in sand-dune and other erosion-prone areas where kelp forests help dissipate waves. Check cleanliness of areas through local knowledge, and organizations such as goodbeachguide.co.uk or Surfers Against Sewage (sas.org.uk).
- Keep records of amounts, and where and when you picked different seaweeds, so you can keep an eye on species varying/changing on different sites, and know where to go for specific species.

* NE has worked closely with the Crown Estate, Cornwall and IFCAs, the National Trust and Cornwall Wildlife Trust to produce a code of conduct for seaweed-harvesting for both commercial and personal use.

Drying and Storing Seaweeds

Traditionally, seaweeds are stored by drying. It's fine to use them fresh, but if you've harvested more than you need immediately, drying is the ideal storage method. Dried sea-

Drying wireweed on a stair banister (left), and sea lettuce on a clothes airer (right)

weeds stored in clean, sealed containers, or hung loosely in well-ventilated areas can keep for up to two years. Thick, darker seaweeds, like kelp, thongweed and wracks, are best kept out of direct sunlight; green weeds (sea lettuce and gutweed) need a dark place to keep their colour. Drying seaweeds requires space, planning and attention. Different-sized seaweeds suit different drying methods.

Drying Techniques and Tips

Wash and clean the seaweeds before drying them. This is tricky with seaweeds such as laver, which will need several changes of water to remove debris, especially if picked from a sandy beach. Brown and longer/larger seaweeds are perfect for hanging on a washing line (on a sunny day), over stair banisters or

Dry small and delicate seaweeds like pepper dulse (top left), carrageen (top right) and gutweed (above left) on clean towels. They dry more quickly than thicker seaweeds like kelp and thongweed (above right)

on a clothes airer. Just ensure there is space for the seaweeds to breathe by regularly turning them. Smaller seaweeds and tips of seaweeds are easier to dry on clean towels or tea towels, or on the lowest temperature (barely warm) in the oven for several hours. Again, move them regularly so they get adequate air and dry properly. Thicker seaweeds will take longer; more delicate ones, like gutweed and pepper dulse, will be quicker. Ex-

When all the moisture has been removed, seaweeds become brittle and friable, and can be flaked or ground, like the laver (top left and right), dulse (above left) and bladder wrack (above right)

pect from one to three days to air-dry thoroughly, and up to 12 hours in a warm oven.

Drying seaweeds for grinding into flakes or powder requires an additional stage. Pliable seaweed doesn't grind well, so heating it at the lowest temperature in the oven, or in a heavy-bottomed pan on the hob, again at the lowest temperature, will remove remaining moisture. It will become brittle and friable – ideal for flakes or powder for certain recipes.

Notes for the Cook

In general, dried seaweeds are very light in weight, so using spoon measurements or electric scales is advisable. All recipes are subject to personal choice, so feel free to adapt to your own preferences.

For Vegans and Vegetarians
Seaweed recipes can completely avoid all animal produce, and you are welcome to create alternatives with appropriate ingredients.

Local ingredients
Cornwall and the IOS have a fantastic choice of fish, seafood, vegetables, salt and milk products, as well as professional seaweed harvesters (the Cornish Seaweed Company). Please do use and enjoy local produce where possible.

Conversions
All measurements are metric. Oven temperatures are for conventional electric ovens. Here are some equivalents:

Oven temperatures
180°C/fan 200°C/350°F/gas 4
200°C/fan 220°C/400°F/gas 6
220°C/fan 240°C/425°F/gas 7
240°C/fan 260°C/475°F/gas 9

Metric/imperial
60 ml	2 fl oz
90 ml	3 fl oz/5 tbsp
125 ml	4 fl oz/7 tbsp
150 ml	5 fl oz/¼ pint
250 ml	9 fl oz
300 ml	10½ fl oz/½ pint
1 litre	1¾ pints
2 litres	3½ pints

Weight
5 ml	1 teaspoon (tsp)
10 ml	1 dessert spoon (dsp)
15 ml	1 tablespoon (tbsp)
8 g	¼ oz
25 g	1 oz
60 g	2 oz
120 g	4 oz
150 g	5 oz
175 g	6 oz
200 g	7 oz
350 g	12 oz/¾ lb
440 g	1 lb
500 g	1 lb 2 oz
600 g	1 lb 5 oz
680 g	1½ lb
1 kg	2 lb 3 oz

Length
2.5 cm	1 in
10 cm	4 in
23 cm	9 in
1 m	39 in/3¼ ft

Seasonal Picking Chart

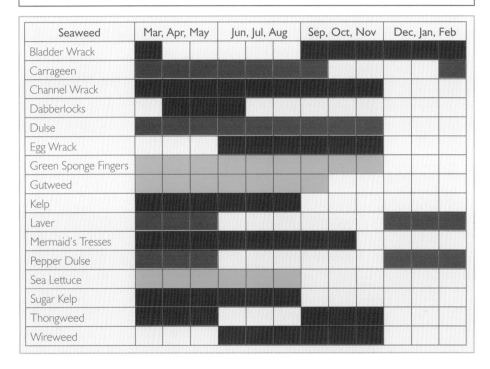

Seaweed	Mar	Apr	May	Jun	Jul	Aug	Sep	Oct	Nov	Dec	Jan	Feb
Bladder Wrack	■						■	■	■	■	■	■
Carrageen	■	■	■	■	■	■						■
Channel Wrack	■	■	■	■	■	■	■	■	■			
Dabberlocks		■	■	■	■	■	■	■	■			
Dulse	■	■	■	■	■	■	■	■	■			
Egg Wrack				■	■	■	■	■	■			
Green Sponge Fingers	▒	▒	▒	▒	▒	▒						
Gutweed	▒	▒	▒	▒	▒	▒						
Kelp	■	■	■	■	■	■						
Laver	■	■	■							■	■	■
Mermaid's Tresses	■	■	■	■	■	■	■	■				
Pepper Dulse	■	■	■							■	■	■
Sea Lettuce	▒	▒	▒	▒	▒	▒						
Sugar Kelp	■	■	■	■	■	■	■	■	■			
Thongweed	■	■	■				■	■	■			
Wireweed				■	■	■	■	■	■			

The seasons and seaweeds are changing, so this chart is a guide only. It aims to assist both the forager and the life cycle of the listed seaweeds by choosing some seasons for picking and avoiding others. Please try to pick only at the times indicated for a particular seaweed. The colours refer to the broad colour categorization of seaweeds: red, green and brown.

Bladder Wrack/Popweed –

Fucus vesiculosus

Where	In a wide variety of settings, from exposed rocky shores to salt water pools
Parts to use	Best to use just the tips; avoid older plants; cut at least 30 cm away from base
Season	Autumn/winter to early spring. Avoid spring/summer – the reproductive season
Nutritional	Contains good amounts of protein and vitamin as well as high levels of phosphorus, bromine, magnesium and iodine. This is one of the main seaweeds used medicinally for iodine deficiency. Vitamin A is highest in the summer, and vitamin C is highest in the autumn

Get the ID right!

- Tough, leathery fronds with air bladders (cylindrical air pockets), normally in pairs either side of a midrib down the centre of the weed. Sometimes the air bladders do not form (for example, in exposed areas)
- Swollen gelatinous tips can form at the end of fronds when reproducing
- Grows up to 90 cm long and 2.5 m wide (though often smaller)
- Black/brown to olive-green in colour

Suggested recipes and uses

Use in pickles, for stock, or simmer and add to salads or fish dishes and stews.

Tips

Just pick the tips to ensure you get the tender parts, leaving the rest intact.

One of the seaweeds that a lot of people know by sight, though not in recipes.

A lightly flavoured seaweed soup. If you can, use homemade chicken stock for an added depth of wholesomeness.

For the stock: Chop up the carcasses as much as possible. Put all the ingredients in a saucepan, cover with 2 litres of water, bring to the boil, and simmer, covered, for 3 hours. Strain and use the stock as follows (this also freezes well for later use).

For the broth: Bring the stock to the boil; add the ginger and bladder wrack, and simmer, covered, for 30 minutes. If using bought/premade stock, remove three-quarters of the bladder wrack now. Add the rice noodles according to packet instructions, followed by the shredded cabbage and finely chopped spring onion in the last minute. Pour over the cooked chicken, reheat gently, and flavour with soy sauce or fish sauce if liked. Serve immediately in warmed bowls.

*If using bought/pre-made chicken stock, add an extra 15g dried bladder wrack, removing excess pieces of seaweed before serving.

Chicken Broth

Ingredients (serves 4)

Chicken stock (makes about 2 litres)
- 1–2 raw or cooked chicken carcasses
- 1 onion, peeled and chopped
- 1 carrot, washed and sliced
- Bunch of parsley stalks
- 2 sticks of celery with leaves, or equivalent in Alexanders, chopped
- 1 tsp mixed dried herbs
- 20 g dried bladder wrack (60 g fresh)
- 2 litres water

Broth
- 1.8 litres chicken stock
- 4-cm length fresh root ginger, peeled and finely chopped
- *5 g dried bladder wrack tips, sliced, or whole if small/tender enough, rehydrated
- 6–8 spring onions, trimmed
- 100 g rice vermicelli noodles
- 100 g shredded green cabbage
- 400 g shredded cooked chicken
- Soy sauce or fish sauce (optional)
- Black pepper, to taste

Pickled Bladder Wrack

Three pickles to choose from, from *al dente* to soft textures.

For the bladder wrack pickle: Wash the bladder wrack tips and pack them into a clean, sterilized jar. Add the spices and garlic. In a small saucepan combine the vinegar, filtered water, sugar (if using) and salt and bring to a boil. Take off the heat and pour over the seaweed in the jar.* Wipe any vinegar spills from the rim with a clean towel and put on the lid. Place in the fridge for 1–3 weeks before using. Can keep up to 6 months.

*Use jars with plastic-lined lids, or line metal lids with greaseproof paper.

For the cucumber and wrack pickle: Follow instructions as above.

For the kohlrabi and wrack pickle: Follow instructions as above.

Ingredients (for 300-ml jar)

Bladder wrack pickle
- 150 g fresh tips (including swollen ends if available) bladder wrack
- 1 tsp spices (mix of mustard seeds, cumin seeds, coriander seeds, black peppercorns)
- 1 clove garlic, peeled and sliced
- 100 ml white wine vinegar
- 100 ml filtered water
- 1 tsp sugar (optional)
- 1 tsp fine sea salt

Cucumber and wrack pickle
- 20 g dried bladder wrack tips (60 g fresh)
- 200 g cucumber, peeled and finely sliced
- 1–1.5 cm fresh root ginger, peeled, finely sliced
- 50 ml white wine vinegar
- 50 ml filtered water
- 25 g Demerara sugar
- 1 tsp fine sea salt

Kohlrabi and wrack pickle
- 250 g kohlrabi, peeled and diced
- 10 g dried bladder wrack (30 g fresh)
- 2 cloves garlic, peeled and sliced
- 100 ml white wine vinegar
- 100 ml filtered water
- 1 tsp fennel seeds
- 1 tsp coriander seeds
- 1 tsp fine sea salt
- 1 tsp sugar (optional)

Pickles, clockwise from bottom left: Cucumber and wrack, kohlrabi and wrack, seaweeds wrack, kohlrabi and wrack

Carrageen/Irish Moss –
Chondrus crispus/Mastocarpus stellatus

Where	Rock pools or on rocks on lower shore, and up to 24 m from high-tide mark. Sheltered and exposed areas, maybe under larger seaweeds. MS more common in exposed locations
Parts to use	All. Leave holdfast intact; use largest plants only
Season	February to early autumn, best in spring/summer (fast-growing season)
Nutritional	CC up to 18 per cent protein. High in calcium, magnesium, zinc, good amount of B12 and iron. Anti-viral and expectorant properties. MS high in vitamin C

Get the ID right!
- 5–20 cm in breadth
- Shaped like a clump of moss, fanned seaweed, branching into two, up to five times
- Burgundy, reddish-brown, purple/almost black (MS) to olive-green (if sun-bleached while growing) in colour; tips of fronds can be iridescent in water
- Fronds of MS curl in, with pip-like bumps on older, fruiting fronds. MS can be tough to touch. CC is soft, and slippery to touch

Suggested recipes and uses
Simmer carrageenan to set panna cotta, pâté, mousse, jelly, ice cream, or to thicken soup.

Tips
Carrageen is traditionally bleached to store it. This entails wetting, letting it dry completely, and repeating the process while it progresses through hues of red and pink to white (see photo, page 14). Bleaching isn't essential, though it tends to neutralize the flavour, and apparently prolongs its shelf life.

Carrageenan is the gelling or setting agent extracted from various red seaweeds. The native and traditional sources of carrageenan in the UK are the red seaweeds *Chondrus crispus* (CC) and *Mastocarpus stellatus* (MS).

Creamy Mushroom Pâté

Ingredients (serves 4)

- 1 small onion, peeled
- 1 clove garlic, peeled
- 125 g mushrooms
- 350 ml whole milk
- 5 g dried carrageen (18 g fresh)
- 1 tbsp vegetable or sunflower oil
- Black pepper (to taste)
- 1 tsp brown or red miso paste

A moreish pâté, with depth of flavour and not a whiff of seaweed!

Finely slice the onion, and chop the garlic. Wash, dry and slice the mushrooms and put aside. In a small pan, bring the milk and carrageen to the boil; lower the heat and simmer for 8 minutes. Meanwhile, in a small frying pan, heat the oil and when it is sizzling add the onion; lower the heat and cook for 3 minutes before adding the garlic, stirring for 1 minute, then the mushrooms, adding black pepper to taste. Cook until the mushrooms soften and the juices start to run.

Strain the milk and carrageen through a jelly bag or fine muslin cloth into a vessel in which you can blend. Put a couple of dessert spoons of the liquid in a shallow bowl. Add a teaspoon of miso to the liquid in the bowl; mix to a smooth paste, and return to the strained milk. Add the mushroom, garlic and onion mix to the liquid, and blend to a rough consistency (or smooth if preferred). Taste, and add more pepper or miso if necessary.

Spoon the contents into two or three ramekins, and allow to cool before refrigerating. Serve from the ramekins, or turn them out on to a plate.* Spread the pâté on toast, crispbread, crackers or oat biscuits. Keeps for a good 5 days in the fridge.

Tip: To loosen the pâté from a ramekin, place the ramekin in a shallow dish of hot water for a few minutes, then carefully cut around the edge of the pâté to loosen, and turn the ramekin upside down on a plate; hold firmly, and with a good shake/s, dislodge the pâté on to the plate.

Losbter Bisque with Carrageen

Ingredients (serves 4)

- 2 500-g lobsters
- 1 onion, peeled
- 1–2 garlic cloves, peeled
- 2 tbsp butter
- 1 tbsp tomato paste
- 125 ml brandy
- 8 g dried carrageen (unbleached)
- Black pepper to taste
- Double cream to serve

The soft texture of carrageen adds a subtle spin to this dish. If using live lobsters, freeze them for 2 hours, to kill them painlessly.

To prepare the lobster bisque: Place the uncooked lobsters in a large pan of boiling water (to cover them), and simmer with the lid on for 14 minutes. Remove the lobsters from the pan (keeping the water), and plunge them into cold water. When cool, remove the meat from the lobster by breaking the tail, and the claws at the joints, and scooping out the meat. Discard the dark intestinal tract from the tail meat. Refrigerate the meat until needed. Smash all the lobster shell into pieces of about 2 cm or smaller. Chop the onion and the garlic; heat the butter in a large saucepan, adding the onion when hot. Lower the heat, and after 3 minutes add the garlic and the lobster shell. Stir regularly for 5 minutes, before adding to the lobster water, along with the tomato paste and brandy. Bring to the boil, cover and simmer for 1½–2 hours , or until it has a strong lobster taste.

To prepare the carrageen: Make sure it is thoroughly dry and crisp. If necessary, you can toast it, by placing in a warm oven, at the lowest temperature, for 30 minutes to ensure all moisture is removed. When dried, grind or blend it to a fine-ish powder.

Back to the bisque: When ready, strain the stock through a fine sieve, checking to make sure no shell has passed through. Put the liquid back in the pan, add the lobster meat in small-flaked pieces, and heat through. Season with salt and pepper to taste. Serve hot, in warmed bowls with a sprinkling of carrageen (about 1 teaspoon on each), and a spoonful of cream. Enjoy with crusty bread.

(Recipe from chef Jonny Mobbs)

Channel Wrack – *Pelvetia canaliculata*

Where	Upper shore, creating a carpet on rocks. Prefers sheltered and rocky areas
Parts to use	All, leaving holdfast in place and leaving percentage of swollen ends if present
Season	Spring to autumn
Nutritional	High in selenium and vitamin C, and good trace elements of other vitamins and minerals

The smallest of the wrack seaweeds, channel wrack is one of those seaweeds I've probably passed without noticing many times, focusing instead on the more commonly eaten seaweeds. The discovery of this wrack has opened up the more subtle flavours of seaweeds to me. Fantastic, as little is needed and it grows abundantly.

Get the ID right!

- 5–15 cm in length, with sides rolled inwards to create channels
- Green/brown to olive-green in colour
- Tough yet smooth texture, brittle when dried out of water, sometimes with swollen fruiting bodies at the forked frond ends

Suggested recipes and uses

Use as a condiment only, to supplement not replace food. Add to quinoa, couscous, rice, mashed potato or salad dressings, and use in omelettes.

Tips

Dry well (see pages 13–15) and grind or flake for use. Alternatively use fresh, chopping finely.

Channel wrack survives well on upper shores with long periods out of seawater. This is due to its small surface area and channels, which help to collect and retain water.

Couscous with Orange and Channel Wrack, and Seaweed Wrack Mayonnaise

Couscous with orange and channel wrack

Ingredients (serves 4)

- 275 g couscous
- 1 tsp fine sea salt
- 10 g (1 heaped tbsp) dried channel wrack, ground
- 400 ml boiling water
- 50 g toasted flaked almonds
- 1 tbsp olive oil
- Grated zest of 2 unwaxed oranges

Seaweed wrack mayonnaise

Ingredients (makes approx. 250 ml)

- 2 organic egg yolks
- ¼ tsp strong mustard
- ¼ tsp fine sea salt
- 2 tsp white wine vinegar
- 10 g (1 heaped tbsp) dried channel wrack, ground
- 175 ml vegetable or sunflower oil
- 50 ml extra virgin olive oil

The couscous (opposite, bottom) is a delicious dish, with a mild background flavour of the sea. The homemade mayonnaise (opposite, top) gives a mineral blast, combined with a subtle seaweed flavour.

For the couscous: Put the couscous, sea salt and channel wrack into a large bowl, pour on the boiling water, cover and leave for 5 minutes. Stir in the almonds, olive oil and orange zest. Serve hot or cold with a beetroot salad, a ratatouille, or a chicken or beef tagine.

For the mayonnaise: Whisk the egg yolks in a bowl, and add the mustard, salt, vinegar and channel wrack, stirring them in together. Next, with the whisk in one hand and the measured oils in a pouring jug in the other, drop by drop whisk in the oil. After about a minute, the mixture should start to thicken; when this happens, start to dribble in the oil a little faster, though not too fast. Continue adding and whisking in the oil; taste and adjust amount of flavourings if necessary. Great as a base in sandwiches, in salads or any way you like to use mayonnaise. Store, covered, in the refrigerator and use within a week.

Dabberlocks — *Alaria esculenta*

Where	Subtidal areas, submerged below the water surface; often only accessible at really low tides. Likes exposed areas, north and west coasts
Parts to use	Leave the holdfast and midrib stem intact, cut lower parts, away from holdfast
Season	Best mid–late spring and early summer. Vitamin B12 highest in late winter
Nutritional	High in calcium, magnesium and good amounts of vitamins C, K and B6, iodine, bromine

A very distinctive, brown seaweed and a member of the Kelp family. Dabberlocks is far more common in Cornwall and the IOS than the better-known Asian version, wakame. It is a lovely firm, yet soft-textured seaweed to use.

Get the ID right!

- A long, brown to olive-green seaweed, with a yellowish midrib stem
- The stem is tough, the fronds are delicate and tear easily (looking a little like a gathered skirt off the main stem)
- Up to 2 m long with claw-like holdfast

Suggested recipes and uses

As a pickle, in salads, or cook as a side vegetable. Use as a wrap for kebabs, and great added to stuffing, baked squash or marrow.

Tips

The midrib is tough, and though it can be used as a food, for sustainability reasons it is preferable to keep the main stem intact and harvest just the 'winged' parts.

Alaria Kimchee and Red and White Sauerkraut

Ingredients (for 1 one-litre Kilner jar)

Alaria kimchee

- 1 kg white cabbage
- 200 g radishes, washed and trimmed
- 1 heaped tsp fresh root ginger, peeled and grated
- 3 cloves garlic, peeled and minced
- 12 g dried alaria (35 g fresh)
- 1½ tbsp fine sea salt
- 1–3 tbsp mineral water (optional)

Red and white sauerkraut

- 650 g white cabbage
- 350 g red cabbage
- 12–20 g dried alaria (40–60 g fresh)
- 1 tbsp fine sea salt

These recipes tap into the health benefits of fermented foods. Kimchee – a spicy, sour relish from Korea (bottom photo, left) – and a colourful twist on sauerkraut from China.

For the alaria kimchee: Wash and thoroughly rinse a one-litre Kilner jar. Finely shred the cabbage, leaving aside one or two of the outer leaves. Grate the radishes, and put into a large bowl with the cabbage, ginger and garlic. If using fresh, carefully slice the alaria off the midrib stem, and slice finely into 5-cm strips. Add these and the sea salt to the bowl. Take handfuls of the mixture, squeezing tightly and releasing any excess liquid into a bowl. Continue until the cabbage is soft and limp (about 10 minutes), and the salt has drawn out some of the liquid. Pack the mixture tightly into the Kilner jar, forcing it down with your fist, and add any liquid drawn from the mixture. Place one or two of the outer cabbage leaves on top, then a weight, such as a clean stone, to help submerge the mixture. Put the jar (with the lid off) in a bowl, and leave for 3–8 days before refrigerating. Keep the mixture covered in liquid, adding a little mineral (not tap) water if necessary and pushing down any floating vegetables, whenever you pass the jar. The mixture will start to ferment, and may overflow into the bowl. Skim off any scum from the surface (a natural part of the process); seal and store. Use as a salad or vegetable accompaniment.

For the red and white sauerkraut: Follow the instructions above. You can add grated beetroot and other vegetables if you like.

Crab and Dabberlocks Salad

Ingredients (serves 4)

- 12 g dried dabberlocks (36 g fresh)
- 4 tbsp rice wine vinegar
- 3 tbsp sesame oil
- 100 g pickled ginger
- 500 g white crab meat
- 1 tbsp lemon juice
- Handful of fresh coriander leaves
- Fine sea salt and black pepper, to taste

A light yet filling salad with zingy flavours.

Chop the seaweed into small pieces and marinade in the vinegar and oil for 30 minutes. Finely slice the ginger and mix in with the crab, lemon juice and coriander leaves, adding the seaweed and marinade when ready. Taste, and add salt and pepper if necessary. Serve immediately, or keep refrigerated for a few hours.

Dulse — *Palmaria palmata*

Where	Loves to grow off kelp stems (*digitata* and *hyperborea*; see photo top left, opposite) on middle to lower shores, including sub-tidal areas down to 20 m. Likes both exposed and sheltered areas
Parts to use	All, leaving holdfast and part of the frond intact
Season	All year round, best spring to autumn
Nutritional	Particularly high in protein, vitamin A and iron, though has good range of other vitamins and minerals, including potassium, B vitamins, calcium and manganese

Get the ID right!
- Red to dark red, flat seaweed with a tough yet thin surface
- Grows normally between 10 and 30 cm long, up to 8 cm wide, with forked, rounded ends
- Often grows in a fan shape, though can be single fronds

Suggested recipes and uses
Delicious added to quiches, pies, fish and potato dishes, or as a condiment added to soups and stews. A simple salad of fresh or rehydrated dulse with lemon is very pleasant.

Tips
Dulse is naturally quite salty, so be careful not to add too much salt to dishes in which you use it.

Perhaps the most nutritious of all seaweeds, in the UK, dulse has traditionally been eaten dried as a snack – just as it is – though it is also very tasty fresh and in numerous dishes (see Suggested recipes and uses).

Sweet Potato Quiche with Dulse

Ingredients (serves 4)

Pastry case
- 175 g flour, ½ brown, ½ white
- 75 g salted butter (room temperature, cubed)
- 5 g dried dulse, ground/flaked (15 g fresh)
- 1–2 tbsp cold water
- A little beaten egg

Filling
- 100 ml whole milk
- 100 ml double cream
- 4 organic eggs (beaten)
- 1 tbsp vegetable or sunflower oil
- 1 small onion, peeled and chopped
- 175 g sweet potato, peeled, small cubes
- 15 g 2-cm pieces dried dulse (45 g fresh)
- ½ tsp fine sea salt (optional)
- Black pepper, to taste
- 40 g feta cheese, cubed

A rich quiche, with dulse instead of bacon.

Grease a 23-cm flan tin with a little butter, and pre-heat the oven to 200°C.

For the pastry case: Rub the flour, butter and ground/flaked dulse together until thoroughly mixed. Add the water, little by little, to form a ball of dough, not too moist. Sprinkle a little extra flour on a clean surface, and roll out the pastry to a circular shape that will fit the tin, including up the sides. Line the tin with the pastry, leaving the edges a little above the sides of the tin, in case of shrinkage. Prick the base of the pastry case with a fork, and brush with a little beaten egg (from the filling). Blind bake for about 20 minutes.

For the filling: Meanwhile, lightly beat together the milk, cream and eggs. Heat the oil in a saucepan or wok, and when hot, add the onion and cook for a few minutes. Add the sweet potato and dulse, and cook, stirring, until the potato starts to soften (about 10 minutes), adding a tablespoon of water to help steam the potato, and a lid to the pan if necessary. Don't let the potato get too soft. Season with salt and pepper if liked. Once the pastry is out of the oven, turn down the temperature to 180/190°C. Spread the potato mixture in the pastry-lined tin. Add the feta, and pour on the egg mixture. Bake for 30–40 minutes, or until firm and set.

Serve warm or cool with a green salad.

Dulse Dukkah Dhal with Stuffed Chapatis

Mild spices three ways. Dukkah is the name for a sesame-seed-based, spiced condiment.

For the dulse spice mix: Dry-roast each of the seeds separately in a medium saucepan over a low heat, stirring regularly so they don't burn. Grind together the roast spices and dried dulse (see photo, page 15).

For the dukkah spice: Grind the sesame seeds separately, add 15 g of the dulse spice mix, salt and pepper. Put aside. (This can also be stored in a clean, dry, lidded jar.)

For the dhal: Chop the tomatoes, and put the flesh aside. Finely chop the onion and garlic; heat the oil and fry over a medium heat until translucent. (Set aside one-third for the chapatis.) Stir in the dulse spice mix; cook for 1 minute, then add the lentils, chopped tomatoes and boiling water. Simmer for 20 minutes, or until the lentils are cooked, stirring regularly. Add a little extra water or salt if needed.

Ingredients (serves 4)

Dhal
- 2 medium tomatoes, skinned
- 800 ml boiling water
- 2 small onions, peeled
- 1 clove garlic, peeled
- 1 tbsp vegetable or sunflower oil
- 20 g dulse spice mix*
- 300 g red lentils, washed
- Pinch of fine sea salt, to taste

Chapatis *(makes 12)*
- 500 g chapati or wholemeal flour
- ½ tsp fine sea salt
- 300 ml cold water
- 175 g cooked, mashed potato (about 1 medium potato)
- 15 g dulse spice mix*
- ½ tsp garam masala
- 1 tsp vegetable or sunflower oil
- 1 tbsp butter (optional)

*Dulse spice mix
- 15 g cumin seeds
- 22 g coriander seeds
- 35 g dried dulse

Dukkah spice
- 15 g sesame seeds
- 15 g dulse spice mix
- Pinch of fine sea salt
- Freshly ground black pepper

For the chapatis: In a bowl, mix 475 g flour with the salt, and gradually add the water to create a soft dough. Knead for 10 minutes until it springs back. To make the stuffing, mix the mashed potato, remaining fried onion and garlic, dulse spice mix and garam masala. Form the stuffing into 12 balls. Divide the dough into 12 and roll each piece into a ball. Sprinkle some leftover flour on a clean surface, roll out one of the dough balls into a 10-cm-diameter circle, put a ball of stuffing in the middle and fold in the edges, pinching them at the top to contain the filling. Roll into a 15-cm-diameter circle. Repeat with remaining stuffing and dough balls. Heat a heavy frying pan over medium heat, and when hot add a chapati and cook for about 1 minute, or until the surface bubbles and brown spots appear; turn and cook the other side for about 30 seconds. Keep warm while you cook the remaining chapatis.

Serve with dhal sprinkled with dukkah, and butter smeared over each chapati.

Egg Wrack — *Ascophyllum nodosum*

Where	Sheltered shores, mainly middle shore on rocks and boulders
Parts to use	Younger tips and younger smaller plants, leaving the holdfast intact
Season	Summer to autumn. Avoid spring reproductive season
Nutritional	A well-rounded source of vitamin and minerals. Includes omega 3 and 6, iodine, and is rich in vitamin C and amino acids. Good amounts of magnesium and zinc. May react with blood-thinners, and in general little research has been done on human consumption of this seaweed, so using as a condiment rather than a vegetable is advised

Get the ID Right!
- Up to 1.5 m long, slender; olive-green to yellow or pale brown
- Tough, leathery texture, with small branches coming off the main stem, and egg-shaped bladders (air pockets) spaced along the main stem
- The branches sometimes have small bladders at the tips

Suggested uses
Dry and grind and use in sweet dishes mixed with sweetener. Use very sparingly.

Tips
Steam or boil before use to bring out a more subtle flavour, especially if using as a dominant flavour. Harvest only very small areas, for this seaweed, particularly older plants, provides a complex habitat.

An unassuming, tough-looking seaweed, with surprising potential. Strongly flavoured.

One bladder on the main stem, plus two years for initial growth, generally equates to one year of growth, and the seaweed itself can live for almost 15 years.

Egg Wrack Sweet and Savoury Snacks

Ingredients (serves 4)

Black olive and egg wrack pâté
- 15 g dried egg wrack (40 g fresh)
- 100 g good black olives (80 g pitted)
- 1 clove garlic
- 1 tbsp capers
- Squeeze of lemon juice
- Extra virgin olive oil (optional)

Seaweed praline
- 200 g dark muscovado sugar
- 10 g/1 tbsp ground dried egg wrack
- 2 tbsp water
- 120 g shelled walnuts

Sweet and savoury snacks incorporating this potent flavour: a rich pâté with a little extra body from egg wrack, and seaweed praline (photo) – a salty, sweet treat.

For the black olive and egg wrack pâté: Soak dried egg wrack for 10 minutes. When ready, cover the wrack (dried or fresh) with fresh water; simmer for 5 minutes, drain and cool. Remove stones from unpitted olives. Put all the ingredients in a food processor, and blend to a rough consistency, adding oil if needed. Serve on toast or with other dips.

For the seaweed praline: Line a large baking tray with greaseproof paper. Put the sugar,

egg wrack and water in a small pan, and stir regularly over a medium heat to dissolve the sugar. Bring the mixture to the boil before turning down the heat and simmering, without stirring, for 10 minutes. Turn off the heat, quickly stirring in the walnuts before pouring the mixture on to the greaseproof paper. Allow to cool for at least 15 minutes, before breaking the praline into pieces and serving in a small bowl.

Store in an airtight container, and enjoy sparingly as a treat.

Green Sponge Fingers/Velvet Horn –
Codium fragile/C. fragile ssp. *atlanticum* (CF and CFA)

Where	Shoreline rock pools, subtidal areas (CFA), or pools rich with coralline algae; mid-lower shore to subtidal 1–2 m. CFA most common across the region; CF across the IOS and south coast of Cornwall
Parts to use	Whole, leaving half the plant and holdfast intact
Season	Spring to autumn
Nutritional	Good iron content and trace elements

The least common seaweed in this book, though, as you'll see, only small amounts are required to make an unusual dish.

There are two types of this seaweed: the Atlantic version (CFA), thought to be native, the other (CF) non-native. Distinguishing the two is tricky without a microscope.

Get the ID right!
- Green to blue/green seaweed, spongy (CFA) or velvety feel
- Branched and 8–45 cm in length (normally up to 20 cm)
- Slightly rounded, blunted tips (CFA); rounded or pointed tips (CF)

Suggested recipes and uses
Use fresh in salads, or in tempura. Cooking extracts a gel-like setting agent for liquids, similar to the function of carrageenan.

Tips
Since CF (*Codium fragile tomentosoides*) is a non-native, invasive species, care should be taken not to spread spores. Follow the 'check, clean, dry' policy (see Seaweed Foraging Guidelines, pages 11–12).

Green Velvet Salad

Ingredients (serves 4 as a side salad)

Salad
- 2 avocados, peeled
- 4 spring onions, trimmed
- 8 cherry tomatoes
- 15 g fresh velvet horn

Dressing
- 2 tbsp cider vinegar
- 1 tsp local honey
- Black pepper, to taste

A mixture of crunchy and soft textures in this funky salad.

Cut the avocados in half, take out the stones, and dice the fruit. Slice the spring onions, and chop some of the fresh stem too. Halve the tomatoes, chop the velvet horn into approximately 2-cm lengths, and gently mix all the ingredients together before dividing into four portions. Combine the cider vinegar, honey and black pepper, and drizzle over each salad. Eat with cold meats, cheeses and bread, or alongside a spicy bean stew with rice or flatbreads.

Gutweed/Sea Greens — *Ulva intestinalis*

Where	Both sheltered and exposed coasts, low to full salinity, upper through to lower shore
Parts to use	Whole length, leaving the holdfast and some fronds intact
Season	Spring and summer – the period of rapid growth
Nutritional	High in calcium and vitamin B12; up to 18 per cent protein, and a good range of other vitamins and minerals

Previously known as *Enteromorpha intestinalis*, the Latin category has been changed to that of Sea Lettuce (page 80). There are several different gutweeds, all tubular.

Get the ID right!
- Tubular, unbranched fronds, inflated by air
- Bright green in colour, sometimes tips are bleached white by the sun
- 2 cm to 70 cm long, the fronds can vary from almost thread-like in width, to up to 15 cm wide

Suggested recipes and uses
Great dried and deep-fried; add fresh or dried to salads and garnishes; dry as a herb for savoury baking (bread, pastry, oatcakes), and powder to add sprinklings over fish, vegetables or meat.

Tips
Gutweed can grow really well at sewage outlets, so double check that your harvesting site isn't one of these. Best to pick from rocky areas, as sand, if it has entered the plant's tubes, is almost impossible to get rid of.

Sea Vegetable Risotto

Ingredients (serves 4)

- 15 ml olive oil
- 25 g butter
- 1 medium onion, peeled and finely chopped
- 200 g courgettes, chopped
- 275 g Italian risotto rice
- 90 ml dry white wine
- 10 g dried, chopped gutweed, plus extra for garnish (approx 30 g fresh)
- 1 litre vegetable stock, hot
- 45 ml double cream (optional)
- 60 g Parmesan, freshly grated
- Black pepper, to taste

A risotto with light green sea vegetables.

Put the oil, butter and onion in a large saucepan, and sauté until golden. Add the chopped courgettes and cook for 1 minute, then mix in the rice and stir to coat grains thoroughly. Sauté for a couple of minutes, until the rice is slightly translucent. Turn up the heat, add the wine and gutweed and let it bubble away, stirring the rice constantly. Now begin to add the stock, a ladleful at a time. When the liquid has been absorbed, add the next ladleful, stirring constantly and adjusting the heat as necessary. If you run out of stock before the rice is cooked, add boiling water and continue cooking. When the rice is *al dente*, take the

pan off the heat; add the cream (if using), Parmesan and plenty of black pepper. Mix well and put the lid on until ready to eat. When serving, add a few strands of sea greens on to each portion as an edible decoration.

Herby Oatcakes with Broad Bean and Sea Greens Dip

Herby oatcakes
Ingredients (makes approx. 20)

- 360 g fine oatmeal (or oats ground in food blender)
- 100 g spelt flour
- ½ tsp fine sea salt
- ½ tsp baking powder
- 5 g (2 tbsp) ground or chopped dried gutweed
- 65 g butter
- 1 egg, beaten
- 60 ml milk or water

Broad bean and sea greens dip
Ingredients (serves 4 generously)

- 1 kg broad beans (250 g shelled)
- 1–2 cloves garlic, peeled
- 60 ml extra virgin olive oil
- Juice of 1 lemon
- 10 g ground or chopped dried gutweed (30 g fresh)
- Fine sea salt and black pepper, to taste
- Mint leaves to garnish (optional)

Delicate sea herbs flavour these companions.

For the herby oatcakes: Pre-heat oven to 200°C, and grease a large baking tray. Mix together all the dry ingredients, and combine with the butter. You can rub in the butter with your hands, or combine the whole lot in a food processor. Add the egg and milk or water and mix for just 3 minutes. The dough should be firm enough to be rolled out; add a little extra liquid if necessary. Roll dough to approximately 3 mm thick, and use biscuit cutters to press out the biscuit shapes. Place on the baking tray and bake for 15–20 minutes. Leave to cool.

For the broad bean and sea greens dip: Take the beans out of the pods and simmer in a medium pan for 2–3 minutes. Strain through a colander and rinse with cold water. Slip the beans out of their grey skins by tearing one end and gently squeezing out the bean. Place in a food processor with the next 5 ingredients and blend, keeping the mixture textured rather than smooth. Adjust flavouring with salt and pepper. Serve fresh, decorated with mint leaves. Will keep for a week in a sealed jar in the fridge.

Kelp/Oarweed/Tangle and Forest Kelp — *Laminaria digitata* and *L. hyperborea*

Where	*Laminaria digitata* is at the farthest extent of the shore, including pools, intertidal and subtidal areas. Paler in colour, *L. hyperborea* is similar, though tends to grow deeper. Both found in exposed and sheltered areas off rocky shores
Parts to use	Cut one or two fronds only from each plant, leaving the holdfast intact
Season	Early low spring tides. Avoid picking after summer, when growth slows down a lot
Nutritional	*Digitata* contains a good range of vitamins and minerals, including B1, 2, 3, 12, calcium, magnesium, and high levels of iodine

Get the ID right!

- Brown, shiny, slippery, leathery surface, belt-like. Slimy edge where freshly cut
- Thick, flexible texture, up to 1.5–2.5 m long and 60 cm wide (at top of the frond)
- Normally divided into 'fingers' – flattened strips

Suggested recipes and uses

For dashi stock for Japanese dishes. Boiled for noodles, added to cooking pulses to reduce both cooking times and flatulence. Fried in squares as a treat.

Tips

The top parts of the fronds, nearest the stem, are the freshest, as this is where the growth happens. The ends are the oldest part.

The main kelps are growing aplenty, though changing climatic patterns imply that this seaweed may be less common in the future.

Kelp forests are important in dissipating waves, and as a habitat for seals and other sea life. Forage sparingly.

Hummus with Kelp

Ingredients (makes 300-g tub)

- 10-cm strip of dried kelp (20 cm fresh)
- 250 g chickpeas, cooked*
- Juice of 1 lemon (3 tbsp)
- 2 tbsp water
- 1 tbsp light tahini
- 1 clove garlic, peeled
- 3 tbsp extra virgin olive oil
- Pinch of fine sea salt

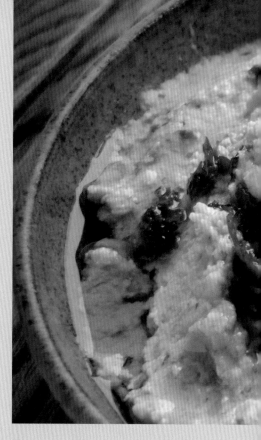

Kelp helps reduce the cooking time and flatulence associated with cooking pulses. It also adds a subtle flavour.

Put the kelp into a small pan, cover with water and simmer for 20–30 minutes. Meanwhile, combine all the other ingredients (except 1 tablespoon of olive oil), and blend until smooth, though not too smooth. Adjust ingredients according to taste and preference. Once the kelp is cooked, blend it separately and add 1 tablespoon of the mix to the hummus. Mix well and spoon into a serving dish. Mix another tablespoon of blended kelp with the remaining tablespoon of olive oil and drizzle over the top of the hummus.

Serve on toast, with crudités, or any way you like. Will keep in the fridge for a week.

*If cooking the chickpeas from dried, you can put the kelp in the cooking pot with them.

This will reduce the cooking time to 30–40 minutes (after soaking first for 8 hours or overnight), and add a subtle flavour. I like to cook extra chickpeas this way, adjusting the amount of kelp accordingly, and once cooked and cooled, freezing what I don't immediately require. Dried chickpeas approximately double in weight once cooked.

Laver/Nori — *Porphyra* species

Where	Lower to mid-shore, up to 15 m subtidal. On rocks, sand, as well as growing off other seaweed species
Parts to use	All, leaving holdfast intact and never stripping a whole rock of laver
Season	Thrives well during winter, until and including spring
Nutritional	High in protein, and a good range of vitamins and minerals, including vitamins B, C, E, and beta-carotene

Get the ID right!

- A fine, translucent seaweed, varying from purple, purple/brown to olive-green
- Can feel like thin plastic (it has a slight bounce when pulled), and looks like sheets of plastic stretched over rocks when dried
- Generally between 20 and 30 cm in length. Can be attached at one end, or in the middle

Suggested recipes and uses

Use in laver 'bread', as a vegetable added to soups, stews, quiche, bread or even sweet dishes such as molasses cookies. Use raw laver in similar ways: torn into pieces for soups or stews, or dried and ground into sweet or savoury baking, or in quick sushi.

A wonderful seaweed, each of the *Porphyra* species has slightly different eating qualities and tastes.

This cold-water genus comprises some 70 species world-wide, of which *Porphyra dioica*, *P. drachii*, *P. linearis*, *P. purpurea*, *P. umbilicalis* and *Pyropia* (formerly *Porphyra*) *leucosticta* are found across Cornwall and the IOS.

Tips

Wash really thoroughly (several times) if picking from sandy beaches. Submerge in a container of water, allow the sand to settle to the bottom and rinse again. Can use as a vegetable rather than just as a condiment. I think raw laver is just as tasty as cooked.

Swirled Laver Bread Loaf

Ingredients

Laver bread*
- Laver (fresh or dried)
- Water

Swirled laver bread loaf *(makes 1 loaf)*
- 400 g strong white flour
- 100 g spelt or wholemeal bread flour
- 1 tsp instant dried yeast
- ½ tsp fine sea salt
- 1 tsp vegetable or sunflower oil
- 150 g cooked laver bread
- 1 tsp honey
- 200 ml warm water
- Little extra flour for rolling

Technically, traditional 'laver *bread*' refers to the black pulp of cooked laver, which makes this a tasty 'laver bread' bread!

*I recommend cooking batches of at least 250 g fresh laver to justify the energy used to cook it. Cooked laver freezes well in an airtight container or sealed bag, for later use.

To make laver bread: If using fresh laver, rinse thoroughly in several changes of water to remove any sand or debris. If using dried, rehydrate for 10 minutes and use the same water for cooking. Place in a saucepan and cover with water – the seaweed will float to the surface, so be careful not to add too much water, and do not attempt to submerge it completely. The goal is for the laver to absorb all the water while cooking. Bring to the boil, cover and simmer for about 3 hours, or until the seaweed breaks down into a pulp. Check and stir regularly to avoid boiling dry, adding a little extra water if required. Liquidize the final pulp to ensure it's broken down into slightly smaller pieces.

For swirled laver bread loaf: Oil a one-kilo loaf tin and put aside. Mix together the flour, yeast, salt, oil and 75 g of cooked laver bread in a large bowl. Dissolve the honey in the water, and gradually stir into the flour mix until you have a workable ball of dough, neither too sticky nor too dry. Knead the dough for 10 minutes, or until it starts to spring back. Place in a bowl, cover and leave in a warm place for 30–60 minutes, or until doubled in size.

Break the dough into two equal pieces. Sprinkle a small amount of flour on to a clean

surface, and roll out each piece of dough into approximately 30 x 10-cm lengths. Spoon the remaining laver bread along the middle of each strip (leaving 2 cm free at the sides and ends). Carefully lift up one end of a piece of dough and start to roll it up, lifting as you go, rather than pushing. Pinch the edges as you go, to ensure the laver stays inside; also pinch the sides once complete, and place roll at one end of the tin. Repeat with the second length, filling the tin. Preheat the oven to 190°C. Cover and leave to rise for a further 30 minutes before baking for 40–45 minutes. Remove from tin, allow to cool and enjoy.

Nori Rice Balls and Rolls

Ingredients (serves 4, makes 32, 8 each)

- 1.2 kg cooked sushi rice (500 g uncooked)

Fillings for 3 kinds of sushi
- 100 g smoked or raw* fish fillets, cut into thin slices or squares
- Cooked prawns (1 per piece)
- Raw vegetables: ½ red pepper, ½ avocado, ¼ cucumber, ½ carrot, sliced in strips
- Squeeze of lemon juice
- 10 g dried laver, ground
- Small bunch of parsley, finely chopped
- 2 tbsp toasted sesame seeds

In Japan, nori is used raw or toasted, not cooked. This alternative to bought nori sheets requires a sushi mat.

Use half the freshly cooked sushi rice, cooled, each for the balls and rolls. Prepare the fillings by finely slicing the red pepper and avocado (adding a squeeze of lemon juice to prevent browning), carrot and cucumber; keep separate. Put the ground laver in a shallow, dry bowl, so it's easy to use.

*Raw fish must be really fresh. Choose types such as cod, mackerel, trout, salmon, sea bass or eel. Ask your fishmonger for 'sushi grade' fish and seafood. Or use smoked fish: haddock, mackerel, salmon or trout.

For the rice balls: You'll need wet hands to handle the rice. Food-grade cling film is useful unless you're experienced at making rice balls. Take 2 tablespoons of rice and place in the centre of a square of cling film; pull in the corners of the cling film to contain the rice, and twist them (squeezing out any air) until you've made a ball of rice. Remove the ball from the cling film with wet hands, and repeat until you have 16 balls, using half the rice. Dip about 12 balls into the laver, covering the top of each ball with seaweed. Continue to decorate these with, for example, a square of fish or a prawn, topping with a small piece of red pepper. Return each ball into the piece of cling film, twisting it again to secure the decoration in place. Garnish with parsley or sprinkles of sesame seeds. Vary the decorations on the balls. For the remaining balls, carefully cut each in half (within the cling film is easiest), sprinkle the cut surfaces with laver, then put the ball back together, retwisting in cling film before decorating, as above.

For the nori rolls: Cover a sushi mat with cling film, wet your hands and spread half the remaining rice across the mat; don't press it down too hard. Using a dry spoon, sprinkle the surface of the rice with a covering of ground laver. Next, arrange your fillings in lines across the laver-covered rice – for example, cucumber, then carrot, then avocado or fish. The lines of fillings should cover about one-third of the whole of the sheet of rice, starting about 2.5 cm from the end of the mat closest to you, and finishing in the centre. Take the closest end of the mat, lift it over the fillings, making an 'n' shape and pressing down to firm up; continue to roll the rice over to the end of the mat. Remove the mat, keeping the cling film in place. Using a wet, sharp knife, neaten the ends of the roll, then cut it into 8 pieces. Remove the cling film and sprinkle individual rolls with sesame seeds. Make a second sushi roll with the remaining rice and fillings.

Mermaid's Tresses/Bootlace Weed –
Chorda filum

Where	Subtidal (always submerged). South coast of Cornwall (possibly across Cornwall) and whole of IOS. Likes pebbled or shelled shores and sheltered areas, including harbours
Parts to use	Whole length (leaving holdfast intact). Use only when fresh, and youngest parts
Season	Spring through to autumn
Nutritional	Contains antioxidants, starch, sugars and trace elements. Moderate in vitamins; high in iodine, boron, bromine and manganese. Has been used as a food for centuries in Japan

Get the ID right!

- Cylindrical weed, up to 8 m long, and each frond is approximately 0.5 cm in diameter
- Covered in light hairs, giving the impression that the weed is inside a translucent membrane
- Brown to olive-brown in colour
- Feels slippery to touch, due to the hairs

Suggested recipes and uses

Add to salads, stir-fry as noodles. Can plait or display in attractive shapes before serving, for a bit of a wow, on the plate.

Tips

Only use fresh, not dried, for food dishes. You can wipe off the slime before using, if you prefer. It is better to use younger tips than older, larger lengths. Its alternative names – Bootlace Weed and Dead Man's Rope – accurately imply that when this seaweed dries out it is great as string, rope or bootlaces.

A lesser-known noodle of the sea, owing to its almost always being submerged below the tide.

Fiery Mermaid Noodles

Ingredients (serves 4 as a small dish)

- 1 large onion, peeled
- 2 cloves garlic, peeled
- 1–2 chilli peppers
- 2 red peppers
- 2–3 tbsp vegetable or sunflower oil
- 400 g fresh mermaid's tresses, washed
- 200 g cooked brown prawns (optional)

A small serving suits this recipe well with its strong flavours.

Finely slice the onion and chop the garlic; de-seed and chop the chilli, and slice and chop the red peppers into chunks. Heat half the oil in a medium-sized saucepan over a medium heat and, when hot, sauté the onion for 2 minutes before adding the garlic and chilli for 1 minute. Add the red peppers, stirring regularly before adding the seaweed. Add the rest of the oil if required. Allow everything to fry well for approximately 3 minutes, or until the seaweed is tender enough to eat. Add the prawns towards the end, if using, ensuring they are heated through thoroughly before serving.

Pepper Dulse –

Osmundea pinnatifida/Osmundea hybrida

Where	Pools and open rock surfaces, sometimes under and attached to larger weeds, middle to lower shore. Other less common variants may be in exposed or sheltered subtidal areas in Cornwall and the IOS
Parts to use	All, leaving the holdfast intact on the rock
Season	All year, best December to May
Nutritional	Rich in minerals, including calcium, magnesium, iron, manganese, copper and zinc as well as up to 8 per cent protein, low in fat and high in fibre. Has a good range of health benefits

Get the ID right!
- 2–10 cm in length
- Flat in shape, or slightly layered branches in *Osmundea hybrida* (false pepper dulse)
- Growing dark in colour (brown-purple) on the lower shore, to greenish-yellow tuft when in sunlight and higher up the shore

Suggested recipes and uses
As an edible decoration to dishes from fried egg to oysters, fish, steak or pork. Use to flavour fish stock or soups.

Tips
Pick with care, as this seaweed is small and tricky to harvest.

Known as flat-fern weeds or rounded-fern weeds. This so-called truffle of the sea is one of the highlights of seaweed flavours.

Potato and Fish Soup with Pepper Dulse

Ingredients (serves 4)

Fish stock

- 1 kg fish bones, heads and tails
- 800 ml water
- 300 ml dry white wine
- 1 onion, peeled and chopped
- 2 bay leaves
- 20 g dried pepper dulse (60 g fresh)
- Freshly ground black pepper
- ½ tsp sea salt

Fish soup

- 2 tbsp butter
- 1 onion, peeled and finely chopped
- 1 leek, trimmed and finely sliced
- 2 tbsp plain flour
- 1 litre fish stock
- 10 g/2 heaped tbsp dried pepper dulse (30 g fresh)
- 450 g small potatoes, peeled and diced
- 400 g white fish (for example, cod, pollack, or haddock), filleted and skin removed, cut into small chunks

A delicious soup using homemade stock.

For the fish stock: Place all the ingredients in a medium-sized pan and bring to the boil. Skim the surface of grey foam, reduce the heat, cover and simmer for 30 minutes, skimming foam occasionally. Strain through a fine sieve and use immediately, or cool and use within 2 days. Can also be frozen until required.

For the fish soup: Melt the butter in a large saucepan over a medium heat. When sizzling, add the onion and leek, stirring regularly for about 3 minutes or until the onion is slightly soft. In a small bowl, mix the flour with a little fish stock – enough to make a smooth paste – then add this to the pan. Stir for 2 minutes, then add the pepper dulse and the rest of the fish stock and slowly bring to the boil. When boiling, lower the heat to a simmer and add the diced potatoes. After 5 minutes add the chunks of fish and cook for a further 5 minutes, or until the fish is only just cooked through and the potatoes are fully cooked. Serve alone or with crusty bread.

Baked Oysters with Burnt Butter Pepper Dulse Sauce

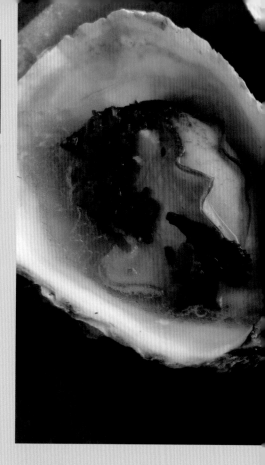

Ingredients (serves 4)

- 16–20 oysters
- 60 g salted butter
- Juice of 1 lemon
- 20 g fresh pepper dulse – about 45 medium pieces (4 g dried)

A simple, effective starter or side dish. You need a few extra oysters to be sure of 4 each.

Preheat the oven to 240°C. Wash and scrub the oysters, place them (curved side down, flat side upwards) on a large baking tray and bake in the hot oven for a few minutes until the shells pop open. Discard any that do not open. Meanwhile, heat the butter over a medium heat, allow to sizzle, cooking for a few minutes until golden. Remove from the heat, then add the lemon juice and pepper dulse, stirring together and putting aside. (If using dried pepper dulse, rehydrate in the lemon juice before adding to the butter.)

When the oysters are open, carefully remove from the oven, discarding the flat oyster tops and keeping the rest of the oyster upright to retain the natural liquid inside the

shell. Holding on to the shell (protect your hands with a cloth or kitchen gloves), gently hook a small, strong, sharp knife under the oyster to cut it from the shell, then arrange the oysters in their shells on plates. Pour over the butter mixture and enjoy immediately, alone or with good bread.

Sea Lettuce — *Ulva lactuca/Ulva rigida*

Where	Often in rock pools, on rocks, stones and other algae. Upper shore to subtidal areas
Parts to use	Whole, leaving behind the holdfast
Season	Best from spring to summer – the fast growing period
Nutritional	High levels of iron, vitamin B12, calcium, protein, magnesium and manganese. Highest amounts of vitamin C in early summer

Looks like a leaf of bright green lettuce. This bright colour means it is easy to spot from quite a distance, which is a great way to impress your friends or family with your foraging skills.

Get the ID right!

- Up to 100 cm across/long, flat or crinkly, often with holes in it, almost translucent
- Bright green in colour, tougher in texture than gutweed

Suggested recipes and uses

Add to bread dough when making, deep fry as crisps, add to ratatouille or stews. Cook lightly and serve as a side vegetable with meat or fish.

Tips

If drying, store in a dark place in order to preserve the wonderful colour. Best to cook or fry, as despite its name, this seaweed can be tough eaten raw.

Sea lettuce is one of the easiest seaweeds to recognize in Cornwall and the IOS, due to its colour and the fact that it grows in accessible areas.

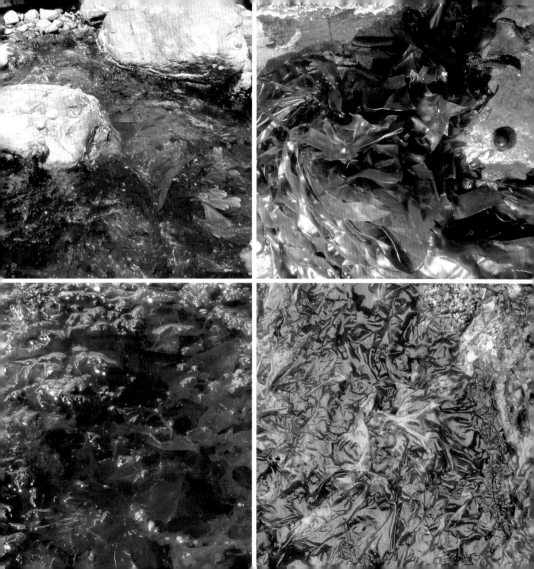

Sea Lettuce Pizza

Ingredients (serves 4)

Base

- 250 g wholemeal flour
- 250 g strong white flour
- ½ tsp fine sea salt
- 5 g (1 tsp) instant dried yeast
- Thyme leaves, finely chopped (2 sprigs fresh, 1 tsp dried)
- 5 g dried sea lettuce (15 g fresh)
- 1 tsp honey
- 325 ml warm water
- Fine polenta

Topping

- 3 tbsp extra virgin olive oil
- 1 large onion, peeled and finely chopped
- 1 clove garlic, peeled and finely chopped
- 400-g tin of tomatoes (blended)
- Thyme leaves (4 sprigs fresh, 1 dsp dried), plus sprigs to decorate (optional)
- 10 g dried sea lettuce, chopped (30 g fresh)
- 1 courgette, finely sliced
- 200 g mozzarella, sliced
- 16 anchovies (optional)
- 50 g Parmesan, finely grated
- A few basil leaves (optional)

Pre-heat the oven to 220°C.

For the base: In a large mixing bowl, combine the flours, salt, yeast, thyme and sea lettuce. Dissolve the honey in the water and slowly add to the flour mix; it needs to be firm, not crumbly or wet. Knead the dough for 10 minutes, then place in the bowl and cover with a clean cloth or cling film. Leave in a warm place for 20 minutes, or until doubled in size.

For the topping: Heat 1 tablespoon of oil in a large pan on a medium heat. When hot, add the onion and stir; cook for 5 minutes or until translucent, adding the garlic in the last 2 minutes. Pour in the tomatoes, thyme leaves (taken off the main stem) and sea lettuce. Bring to the boil and simmer for 10 minutes.

When the dough has risen, divide into four equal balls. Lightly sprinkle a clean surface with polenta, and roll out each ball to about 20 cm in diameter, leaving it slightly thicker at the edges. Spread the tomato mix on to the pizza bases, leaving 2 cm free around the edge. Layer with courgette, mozzarella and anchovies; top with parmesan, basil leaves and a drizzle of oil. Sprinkle a large baking tray with polenta, place a pizza on it and bake for 15 minutes. Repeat with the other three.

Sea lettuce pizza: a great and tasty way to incorporate nutritional seaweed into familiar recipes

Honey-roasted Seaweed

Ingredients (serves 4 as a snack)

- 3 tbsp (60 g) honey
- 2 dsp (20 ml) vegetable or sunflower oil
- 3 tbsp (45 ml) water
- 50 g salted, roasted pistachio nuts (in shells)
- 15 g (very large handful) dried sea lettuce
- 40 g pumpkin seeds

A beautifully sweet, though not too sweet, salty though only slightly salty, chewy, crispy seaweed treat!

Pre-heat the oven to 160°C, and line a large baking tray with baking paper.

Heat the honey, oil and water in a small pan, bring to the boil and simmer for 5 minutes to reduce the liquid a little. Meanwhile, remove the pistachio nuts from their shells, and rub off any of the skin that you can. Roughly crush the pistachios under the flat of a knife blade – just enough to break them up, but do not pulverize them.

Cut the sea lettuce into approximately 2.5-cm pieces. Over a very low heat, add the sea lettuce, pistachio nuts and pumpkin seeds to the honey mixture. Stir thoroughly. Ensure the whole mixture is covered with the honey

water. If there seems to be a bit of excess liquid in the pan, keep stirring until it is absorbed; if not, turn off the heat.

With a wooden spoon, spread the mixture evenly on to the baking paper, and bake in the middle of the oven for 30–35 minutes. Take out and cool. Break into pieces, and if not eating immediately, store in a clean, airtight container. It will keep for several weeks.

Sugar Kelp/Poorman's Weather Glass

— *Saccharina latissima*

Where	Subtidal areas, also pools and gullies in rocky and unstable/disturbed areas
Parts to use	The frond only, leaving the stipe (stem) and holdfast intact on the rock
Season	Spring and summer, avoid in autumn and winter
Nutritional	High in iodine, with good amounts of calcium and magnesium, as well as a range of other vitamins and minerals

A salty-sweet, light type of kelp. I find sugar kelp the hardest seaweed to forage for from the shore, due its preference for subtidal growing environments.

Get the ID right!

- Typically 1.5 m in length, single fronds which can be up to 4 m long
- A brown to yellowish-brown seaweed, with what looks like a frilly, crumpled edge to a deeply dimpled seaweed
- A thin stipe (stem), only 60 cm long, that attaches the weed to the holdfast

Suggested recipes and uses

Add sparingly into desserts, biscuits and even soups and stews, including with other kelps.

Tips

If you want to know if moisture is in the air, or indeed on its way, hang a piece of sugar kelp outdoors. It will stay dry and brittle or go limp, hence predicting the weather to come.

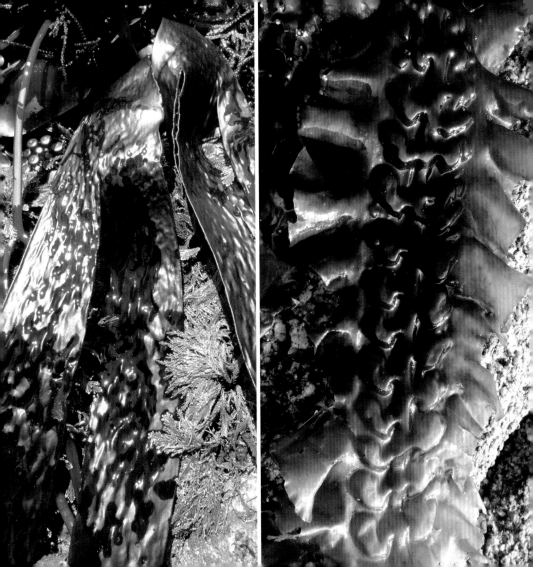

Spicy Apple Turnovers with Sugar Kelp and Carrageen Ice Cream

Ingredients (makes 8, serves 4)

Spicy apple turnovers

- 1–2 g/1 dsp dried sugar kelp, ground (6 g fresh, finely chopped)
- 2 whole cloves
- 1 cm cinnamon stick
- 2 tbsp water
- 30 g dates, pitted and chopped
- 200 g eating or cooking apples, chopped
- 2 tbsp vegetable or sunflower oil
- 4 sheets filo pastry

Carrageen ice cream

- 550 ml whole milk
- 500 ml double cream
- 1 vanilla pod
- 100 g unrefined sugar
- 10 g dried, bleached carrageen

Soft and crispy textures in these light turnovers, with a perfect seaweed ice cream.

Preheat the oven to 180°C.

For the spicy apple filling: Grind the sugar kelp, cloves and cinnamon stick with a heavy pestle and mortar or spice grinder, and place in a small saucepan with 2 tablespoons of water. Add the dates, then the apple, peeled. Cook for a few minutes over a medium heat, with the lid on, until all the water has been absorbed. Keep a close eye on the pan, to stop it boiling dry. When ready, remove from the heat, keeping the lid on until ready to use.

For the turnovers: Pour the oil into a small bowl and lightly oil a baking tray. Lay out one sheet of filo pastry, brush it with oil (a pastry brush is useful) and lay another sheet on top, brushing with oil. Cut the layered sheets into four lengths and, starting with the first length, place one tablespoon of apple mixture 2 cm from the end. Fold the pastry over at an angle (in a triangle shape), and continue to fold to the end of the length to create a turnover. Repeat with all of the lengths, then repeat the whole process with the remaining two filo sheets. Place on the baking tray, brush the tops with the remaining oil and bake for 25 minutes, or until light golden brown. Enjoy warm or cold with ice cream.

For the ice cream: Put all the ingredients into a medium-sized pan, bring to the boil and simmer for 15 minutes. Strain through a jelly bag (don't squeeze; use what easily comes through). Put in a 600-ml lidded plastic freezer box, and allow to cool, or in an ice cream maker. If using a box, freeze the ice cream for 1 hour, remove, mash and refreeze; repeat 3–5 times, or until fully frozen. Remove from the freezer 20 minutes before serving.

Thongweed/Sea Spaghetti –
Himanthalia elongata

Where	Grows on the lower shore from rocks
Parts to use	The length of the seaweed, not the button, cut one of each pair of fronds
Season	Spring and autumn. Harvest after summer reproductive season if possible
Nutritional	Good range of vitamins, minerals and trace elements. Good for calcium and magnesium

A fantastic, flat noodle, grown by the sea and easy to use.

Get the ID right!

- Long, flat lengths, looks like flat noodles, up to 1–2 m long
- Each length splits, or forks into two, hence the name thongweed
- Olive-green, brown to yellowy brown in colour
- The base of the weed is a small (1–2 cm across), rubbery disc (looks like a button) attached to the rock; the weed grows from its centre

Suggested recipes and uses

Add into soups or stews in small strips, cook like spaghetti, or cook *al dente* and chop into salads. Young shoots can also be used raw, finely chopped in salads.

Tips

Don't be shocked when the water turns brown when cooking, this is normal! The stock can also be mixed with ginger, miso and vegetables to make a broth-like soup.

Pan-fried Fish with Sea Spaghetti

Ingredients (serves 4)

- 2 dsp (20 ml) dark soy sauce
- 2 dsp (20 ml) sweet chilli sauce
- 4 fish fillets, 750 g (cod, pollack, hake or turbot)
- 60 g dried thongweed (180 g fresh)
- 700 g leeks, trimmed
- 100 g chard or spinach, washed
- 4-cm piece fresh ginger, peeled
- 2 cloves garlic, peeled
- Fine sea salt and black pepper, to taste
- 3 tbsp vegetable or sunflower oil
- 8 cherry tomatoes, quartered
- 160 g rice sticks (flat noodles)

A complex dish, which is truly a meal in itself.

Mix together the soy sauce and sweet chilli sauce. Lay the fish fillets in a large flat dish, and use half the sauce mixture to massage into each fillet, both sides. Leave the fish to marinade for at least an hour.

Cut the thongweed into noodle-lengths and, if dried, soak in cold water for 10–30 minutes. Clean and slice the leeks, discarding any tough outer leaves. Remove and discard the stems from the chard or spinach and chop the leaves. Finely chop the ginger and garlic. Heat 1 tablespoon of oil in a wok or large frying pan over a medium heat, and fry the leeks and ginger for 5 minutes. Add the chard or spinach leaves, tomatoes and garlic, season with salt and pepper, and cook for a further 3 minutes, or until all is soft and slightly charred.

Meanwhile, bring the thongweed to the boil in a large pan and simmer for 15 minutes (till soft, or less if you prefer slightly *al dente*). Add the rice sticks according to packet instructions (normally after 7 minutes), strain through a colander and put aside. While the rice sticks are cooking, remove the cooked leek mix from the wok or pan, add 2 tablespoons of oil on a medium heat and fry the fish for 3 minutes on each side (skin-side down first), or until cooked and the flesh easily breaks away. Remove and keep warm.

Just before serving, return the noodles to the pan, pour in the remaining marinade and heat through. Serve with the vegetables, and the fish placed on top of each portion.

Seaweed Tempura with a Wild Dipping Sauce

Ingredients (serves 4 as a snack)

Tempura
- 60–100 g fresh or rehydrated thong-weed
- 75 g plain flour
- 1 tbsp cornflour
- Pinch of fine sea salt
- 1 egg, beaten
- Vegetable or sunflower oil for frying
- 200 ml ice-cold sparkling water

Dipping sauce
- 1 tbsp dark soy sauce
- Juice of ½ lemon
- Foraged black mustard flowers to decorate (optional)

Sweet, salty, crispy and soft – a wonderful deep-fried treat with so much going for it.

For the tempura: Pat dry the seaweeds in a clean cloth to remove excess water, and cut them into smaller pieces. Prepare the tempura batter by combining flours, salt and egg. Meanwhile, in a medium saucepan heat 2.5 cm depth of vegetable or sunflower oil to almost smoking. Have a couple of plates with kitchen towel on nearby, to absorb excess oil. At the last minute, add the sparkling water to the tempura batter and briefly mix: it is better to have lumps in the batter than to over-mix it.

When the oil is ready, using tongs carefully dip the seaweeds one by one into the batter then into the hot pan.* Do not over-crowd the pan. Fry for 1–2 minutes, or until golden brown; remove with a slotted spoon on to the kitchen towel. Repeat with all the seaweed.

For the dipping sauce: Mix the soy sauce, lemon juice and mustard flowers in a ramekin or small bowl.

Enjoy the tempura hot or cold with the dipping sauce.

*Hot oil is dangerous, a mesh splatter guard is recommended to protect you from potential hot, spitting oil. Do not leave hot oil unattended.

Wireweed — *Sargassum muticum*

Where	Rock pools and areas between tides (subtidal areas). Shallow water and sometimes estuarine waters
Parts to use	All, though branches off the main stem are most tender. Leave holdfast in place
Season	Summer and autumn
Nutritional	Good range of vitamins and minerals, particularly magnesium, calcium and potassium; low iodine (lowest of brown seaweeds)

A light-coloured seaweed with a simple and pleasant taste.

Get the ID right!

- A brown to olive/pale-brown seaweed, grows up to 2 m long
- Has smaller branches off the main stem, with small air bladders (that effectively look like peas), and even small 'leaves'

Suggested recipes and uses

Use in salads, or grind or chop into stews or stir-fries. Can also be dried whole and rehydrated, or dried and ground before adding to condiments.

Non-native and invasive, sargassum first came to the British Isles in the 1970s. Now common in Cornwall and the IOS, it is considered by some as the sea equivalent of Japanese knotweed. Sargassum is self-fertile and competes with green seaweeds for growing environments. I don't like labelling plants or seaweeds as a pest or bad – everything has value. Sargassum is rich in minerals, so eating it is a great way to dispose of it. Follow the 'check, clean, dry' guidelines (pages 11–12).

Tips

This seaweed absorbs up to ten times its weight in water, so only small amounts are needed for eating. That is why it has been suggested as a nutritionally rich slimming aid: it fills you up and has a good nutritional range. Cutting and using the side branches off the main stem will ensure you use the tenderest parts. Follow the 'check, clean, dry' policy (see Seaweed Foraging Guidelines, pages 11–12).

Smoky Stir-fry

Ingredients (serves 4)

Egg-fried rice (optional)
- 250 g brown basmati rice
- I egg, lightly beaten
- I tbsp sesame oil
- I tbsp vegetable or sunflower oil

Smoky stir-fry
- 15 g dried wireweed, chopped or ground (45 g fresh)
- 150 ml boiled water
- I bunch spring onions, trimmed, or I onion, peeled
- I clove garlic, peeled
- 300 g carrots, peeled
- 100 g chard, spinach or sea spinach
- I tbsp vegetable or sunflower oil
- I heaped tsp Cornish Smoked Sea Salt
- 100 g fresh peas (shelled)
- Black pepper, to taste

Keep it simple, so the flavours come through. A perfect side dish, or main with egg-fried rice.

For the egg-fried rice: In a large pan, bring to the boil 600 ml of water. Add the rice, and turn down the heat before putting on the lid and simmering for 25 minutes. Once cooked, turn off the heat, but do not remove the lid.

Mix together the egg and sesame oil, and heat the vegetable or sunflower oil in a large saucepan, until almost smoking. Add the cooked rice and cook for 3–4 minutes, stirring regularly. Briskly stir in the egg mix with a wooden spoon, leave for 30 seconds and take off the heat. Cover and keep warm while you make the stir-fry.

For the smoky stir-fry (photo opposite): If using dried wireweed, cover with boiling water and leave for 10 minutes. Meanwhile, finely chop the spring onions and garlic, and slice the carrots lengthway into matchsticks. Cut the stalks off the chard, spinach or sea spinach. Heat the oil in a large frying pan or wok and, when hot, add the onion and garlic and sweat for 2–3 minutes over a medium heat. Stir in the carrot sticks, stems of chard, spinach or sea spinach and salt; fry for about 4 minutes, then add the rehydrated wireweed and water, vegetable leaves and the peas. Cook for 10 minutes, stirring regularly until the carrots are soft. Season with black pepper. Serve hot with the rice.

Carrot and Sargassum Salad

Ingredients (serves 4 as a side salad)

Salad
- 2 medium carrots, washed and trimmed
- 12 g fresh wireweed sprigs

Dressing
- 1 tsp dried, ground wireweed*
- 1 heaped tbsp crème fraîche
- Squeeze of lemon, to taste

A light and refreshing salad, continuing the theme of carrots and wireweed.

For the salad: Peel the carrots into fine strips, using a toothed vegetable peeler, or do this carefully with a knife. Arrange on a plate with the sprigs of wireweed.

For the dresing: Mix the ingredients. Serve with the salad, as an accompaniment to mezze, Indian or Mexican dishes.

*To grind the wireweed, use both the tough stems and the finer branches. The plant must be thoroughly dried first. Use a heavy pestle and mortar, or a good electric seed grinder.

References and Further Reading

Allen, Darina (2009), *Forgotten Skills of Cooking: The time-honoured ways are the best – over 700 recipes show you why*, London: Kyle Cathie

Bailey, L, & Owen, K. (2014), *Seaweed Harvesting: Natural England's Advice*, UK: Natural England (enquiries@naturalengland.org.uk/Tel 0300 060 3900)

Brodie, J., Williamson, C., Smale, D.A., Kamenos, N.A., Mieszkowska, N., Santos, R., Cunliffe, M., Steinke, M., Yesson, C., Anderson, C.M., Asnaghi, V., Brownlee, C., Burdett, H.L., Burrows, M.T., Collins, S., Donohue, P.J.C., Harvey, B., Foggo, A., Noisette, F., Nunes, J., Ragazzola, F., Raven, J.A., Schmidt, D.N., Suggett, D., Teichberg, M., & Hall-Spencer, J.M. (2014), *The Future of the Northeast Atlantic benthic flora in a high CO2 World*, W. Sussex: Ecology & Evolution: John Wiley

Brodie, J., Wilbraham, J., Pottas, J., Guiry, M.D (2015), 'A revised check-list of the seaweeds of Britain', *Journal of the Marine Biological Association of the United Kingdom*, Cambridge: Cambridge University Press

Bunker, Francis; Brodie, Juliet; Maggs, Christine and Bunker, Anne (2012), *Seaweeds of Britain and Ireland*, Plymouth: Wild Nature Press

Examine.com (2011–15), *Ascophyllum nodosum*, www.examine.com. Scientific research into supplement benefits

Houston, Fiona and Milne, Xa (2008), *Seaweed and Eat It: A Family Foraging and Cooking Adventure*, London: Virgin Books

Lambert, Rachel (2015), *Wild Food Foraging in Cornwall and the ISles of Scilly*, Penzance: Alison Hodge

Mabey, Richard (2012), *Food for Free*, London: Collins

Madeira, Crystal J. (2007), *The New Seaweed Cookbook: A Complete Guide to Discovering the Deep Flavors of the Sea*, Berkeley CA: North Atlantic Books

Maher, Neil (2011), Dr Maher's Seaweed Sensations, www.seaweed-sensations.com. Information on and supply of seaweeds

Morrissey, J., Kraan, S., & Guiry, M. D. (2001), *A Guide to Commercially Important Seaweeds on the Irish Coast*, Dublin: Bord Iascaigh Mhara/Irish Sea Fisheries Board, www.academia.edu

Mouritsen, Ole; Johanse, Mariela; Mouritsen, Jonas Drotner (2013), *Seaweeds: Edible, Available, and Sustainable*, Chicago: University of Chicago Press

Natural History Museum (2016), Big Seaweed Search, London: www.nhm.ac.uk

Power, Marie (2013), *The Sea Garden: A Guide to Seaweed Cookery and Foraging*, Co Waterford: The Sea Gardener

Rhatigan, Prannie (2009), *Irish Seaweed Kitchen: The comprehensive guide to healthy everyday cooking with seaweeds*, Holywood NI: Booklink

Surey-Gent, Sonia, and Morris, Gordon (2000), *Seaweed: A User's Guide*, Surrey: Whittet Books

The Seaweed Site:
http://www.seaweed.ie/. General information on all aspects of seaweeds.

Wright, John (2009), *Edible Seashore: River Cottage Handbook No. 5*, London: Bloomsbury

Yesson, C., Bush, L.E., Davies, A.J., Maggs, C.A., and Brodie, J. (2015), 'The distribution and environmental requirements of large brown seaweeds in the British Isles', *Journal of the Marine Biological Association of the United Kingdom*, Cambridge: Cambridge University Press

Cornish Suppliers

- **The Cornish Seaweed Company:**
  http://cornishseaweed.co.uk/. Organic, sustainably sourced Cornish seaweeds
- **Cornish Sea Salt Company:**
  http://www.cornishseasalt.co.uk/. Cornish sea salt, hand-harvested from marine protected waters

Foraging Courses and Walks

Rachel Lambert offers accessible, hands-on foraging experiences for all ages and levels of experience. Find out more on her website: http://www.wildwalks-southwest.co.uk/

Acknowledgements

I should like to thank the following:
Juliet Brodie (Natural History Museum), for sharing her expertise and relevant publications on seaweeds in Cornwall and the Isles of Scilly; the Crown Estate and Natural England, for their input into legalities and sustainability surrounding seaweed foraging; Britta James for her loan of pots and crockery; Miles Lavers (Foodswild) and Dr Neil Mahers (Seaweed Sensations), for their knowledge of using seaweed as food; and all the friends, colleagues and students who have trialed and shaped the recipes. Finally, thanks to my publisher, Alison Hodge, for accepting and supporting the idea, and to Yvonne Bristow, the food editor, who strongly encouraged the creation of this book.

Photo credits